SACRED GEOMETRY CELLS

Unleash Your Creative Symmetry

Alexis Zachary

Table of Contents

CHAPTER ONE 2

   INTRODUCTION...2

   MATERIALS FOR ENLIGHTENING EXERCISES 3

   LITTLE BY LITTLE HEADINGS TO MAKE MATHEMATICAL MODELS...7

CHAPTER TWO 10

   THE MOST IDEAL WAY TO MAKE OR PICK A BLEND PLAN...10

   USING POSITIVE AND NEGATIVE SPACE........................13

   BY AND BY HEADING GUIDELINES TO COMBINATION YOUR GAME PLAN 16

CHAPTER THREE 21

   STRIP OR SPOTTED 21

   EXAMPLES OF MATHEMATICS IN STYLE........................22

   NUMERICAL GAME-PLAN SHAPES FOR BRAND CHARACTER STRUCTURES...24

   BRAND LOGO PLAN WITH CLEAR MATH 26

NUMERICAL MODELS FOR THINGS AND PACKAGING 27

USE EVALUATION IN DECREASED APPLICATIONS AND SITE PLAN 28

HOW MIGHT YOU MAKE MATHEMATICAL MODELS FOR YOUR PLANS ON ENHANCE? 33

CHAPTER FOUR 36

HOW MATHEMATICAL OUTLINES MAKE ARRANGEMENT MODELS 36

NUMERICAL NEGATIVE SHAPES 41

THE END 43

CHAPTER ONE

INTRODUCTION

Numerical Cells Model Today, I'll let you know the most effective way to draw this numerical cells plan thoroughly using the most notable saw method. Generally, you will require a couple of design or spotted paper and several markers that adhere to the standards, which are crucial for teens to follow. We should start managing this system thinking about science; I truly need to thank you for thinking about drawing it.

MATERIALS FOR ENLIGHTENING EXERCISES

1. Spotted paper (Tsuki or Leuchtturm1917).

2. A pencil (Bruynzeel or MUJI-style).

3. Faint fine liners (Sakura Pigma Micron).

4. Variety markers like the Sakura Pigmy Brush and Fabric color: Get 10% off and free general store visits on related items with the code MARIO10. Notwithstanding, to find a standard book with direction for each step, continue to look.

Step 1: Sketch a rectangular connection. Draw a rectangular cross segment with any pencil. This will give you a striking outline in the beginning stages to hold the piece back from setting up. Each square shape should be 5 contacts wide x 6 spots tall. These related lines will be cleared out from here on out.

Step 2: Make little jewels. Grab a dull fine liner (I used a Sakura Pigmy Micron 01) and draw immaterial monster stone shapes around the connection's mixes. Regardless, as there are virtually all additional stones, try to leave a free connection point between each essential stone and the one that goes with it.

Step 3: Sketch hexagons. Draw these colossal hexagons around the flood blends in with the dull fine liner you used in the past step. Use the contacts as a sort of point of view.

Step 4: Make the outlines thicker. Pick a thicker nib (I used a Sakura Pigma Micron 05) and embrace the shapes you've drawn in at this point. This will make the shapes stick out and make the model stand isolated perpetually out more. The pencil structure you started with can now be taken out.

Step 5: Draw cell-like shapes. Use a general nib to by and large figure out for the numerical shapes. Draw spots and standard shapes inside the fundamental stones and hexagons. Make sure that everyone is very clear to show that they are real cells. You can similarly work with another shape for such headway.

Step 6: Plan the hexagons. Utilize spread lines to occupy in the space between the standard shapes and the hexagons with a fine line with a basic hint (I utilized a Sakura Pigmy Micron 01). You can wreck around and make them somewhat wavy in the event that you don't keep them totally straight.

Step 7: Play with it. Get a few camouflaged pencils! Make a couple of masses and spot them in the cells. You should allow yourself a few extra jerks of space around them because they shouldn't perfectly match that cell shape.

The Sakura Pigmy Brush gave me two particular tones, orange and purple; In any case, you can involve any a few tones in any request.

Step 8: Notice the shapes. Utilizing vertical lines embellish the enormous stones and hexagons in regions with the thicker fine liner (for my circumstance, Micron 05).

LITTLE BY LITTLE HEADINGS TO MAKE MATHEMATICAL MODELS

Various copies of the seed of life plan, or essentially more, the adolescent of life, are utilized in my standard model. In this creation, a solitary focal circle impeccably interfaces all of the six circles. A portrayal of the seven days of creation can be found at the characteristic of association of the picture of life in sprout. The best degree of information and understanding is the adolescent of life, and it is connected with various head and serious things.

What You'll Need

1. Compass (preferably with the ability to change the pencil/pen)

2. Protractor (for making approaches that don't have six lines of balances)

3. Pencil and eraser

4. Set of pens (with a level of groupings)

5. Old diary or scrap paper

6. Stabile felt-tip pens

The tones are according to a general point of view impeccable. While picking pens to use for such exercises, I see that the tips are phenomenally fine as well as totally dazzling for disguise. A thicker, hazier pen: This will be utilized to drive your arrangement or figure out the negative space/head foundation.

CHAPTER TWO

THE MOST IDEAL WAY TO MAKE OR PICK A BLEND PLAN

While picking a blend plan, attempt to take a gander at tones or tones that are near one another in the light reach. Mix Appear at Joins Ordinarily as One (Following the Rainbow)

1. Red

2. Orange

3. Yellow

4. Green

5. Blue

6. Indigo

7. Violet

8. (Pink)

They appear at rehashes and changes to red after the pink. I propose utilizing transitory tones, like the fragment among green and blue. Assuming you figure the strategy ought to have an even slant, use colors that are near each other. Change from hazier to lighter or the opposite perspective for getting around for highlighting covers. Negative space is the "nothingness" in a plan. Arrangement Appear at Blend Hazier Variety Going to or Coming From Lighter Tone Red, Orange, Yellow, Blue, Green, Yellow, Pink, Purple,

Blue, Dull White. Weak Contrasting Game plan Matches Red, Orange, Yellow, Blue, Green, Yellow, Pink, Purple, Blue, Faint White. Weak reliably rules to utilize positive and negative space I utilize high detachment to make negative space, or the Vesica Pisces, between the fledgling petals, subject to the procedure. I find that the use of negative space helps with drawing out the arrangement and its tones. Positive space is the central sign of relationship of the framework and is where I reliably use astounding groupings.

USING POSITIVE AND NEGATIVE SPACE

The Seeds of Standard Plans in various Seeds of Lives Monique Making the Seed and Bloom of Life.

1. Put a pencil in the compass. Guarantee the compass' tip is level with the pencils.

2. Close the surveyed ideal circle. Pick the best size for your framework. The more straightforward the circle, the harder it is to draw.

3. Place an old scratch pad or piece of paper under your compass with the goal that it doesn't move while you're drawing.

4. Pick a section start on your paper, whether it's the center or more like a corner, and draw the central circle.

5. Along the edge of the circle, pick a segment draw the going with circle, and draw it.

6. Draw another circle where the two circles meet, until there are six circles that coordinate your middle circle. Supersede the pencil in the compass with a pen, and follow over the strategy to make it obvious while covering it. Following five minutes, kill the pencil marks as the ink should have dried. Getting by Seed in a Living Seed Return to the trait of relationship in your framework and make a tremendous circle along it. Try to make the more prominent,

more unmistakable circle near the edges of the seriously unpretentious, less unquestionable external circles. Go to the edge of the more clear circle while keeping up with the size of a vague circle and plant another life seed. While drawing the more key seed of life, stop at the edge with the objective that the more straightforward arrangement stays in a specific piece. Remove the pencil from the compass and, using a pen, trace over the blueprint to make it visible while concealing it. Following five minutes, erase the pencil marks.

BY AND BY HEADING GUIDELINES TO COMBINATION YOUR GAME PLAN

1. Pick a structure plot that you really need to use. Along these lines, pick a region for your negative space.

2. If you really have any desire to have negative space in your framework, carefully mark the space with a pencil.

3. Starting at the lightest or haziest arrangement in your event plot, begin hiding and work your way out. To make your plan stick out, give each layer a substitute tone with a sluggish change from some unique choice from what a large number individual would consider

possible or elective varieties that are specific from one another.

Example: The Vesica Pisces between the essential circle and the layer that comes after it are orange, and the Vesica Pisces in the point of convergence of the circle are yellow. Blend your game-plan how you could need to, and appreciate. It has been shown that imaginative psyche is an exceptional type of pressure alleviation that is authentic for your psychological prosperity. What are the Seed and Sprout of Life? Each culture and religion on the substance of the earth ought to have the decision to see the seed of life. Maybe of the most honored and captivated number in the world, the number seven, is facilitated by the seven interlocking circles that make up a six fold worth.

1. The Vesica Pisces structure, which appears to be a six-pointed star, provides support for the supporting juvenile. The Vesica Pisces is a mathematical shape that is made by the mix points of two covering circles with a questionable reach.

2. The bloom of life is the most amazing, out-of-date image that has ever been observed anywhere on Earth. It supposedly is the diagrams for the universe, and its key game plan fills in as the procedure for all that exists. In this way, obviously life contains a record of every single living thing and the mysteries of the universe. Inside, numerical models

There is a lot of inspiration to be stressed over the numerical model, paying little heed to what style the space is tuned to. It can be used in modern, particularly arranged retro or ethnic styles. Mathematical models are by and by unprecedented while dealing with a space. It isn't central to pick basically blossom or fair-minded models. There has never been a more crucial point in time to blend the models. You totally need to stick to using numerical models while merging various subjects. The model is faltering and stands secluded the most through a monochrome establishment and furniture. The mathematical model will likewise stress critical strong regions for and. It mixes perfectly with persevering through fine art or works of contemporary craftsmanship. With only one stunning upset in the room, it impeccably meets exquisite essentials. The astounding model is the chevron. The chevron, otherwise called fishbone in this nation, is an astounding that is certainly turning into a model. It is a mix plan that commonly substitutes two extra unprecedented, made senses of varieties. It is feasible to join different collections, yet totally the puzzle should be remained mindful of. Chevron is an apparent and wonderful model. It is sufficient to energize a piece of the room with an unsettled in a crisscross plan a shade, a piece of the wall, a cover sprinter, and so on to beautify within.

CHAPTER THREE

STRIP OR SPOTTED

A stripe is an excellent among all gems. From now forward, endlessly apparently everlastingly, the stripe has stood firm on a famous foundation in plan. Style and plan experts are taught in its application. It gives it a parkle and non-abrasiveness, is youthful, and flawlessly spices up the inside. On the off chance that you genuinely want to clearly foster the space utilizing level stripes, the stripe can be a huge stunt. Vertical stripes will be used to foster the walls. Spotted is tomfoolery and perky. It can add a stunning sprinkle of retro when picked in the right degrees. The best option for animating is this one.

EXAMPLES OF MATHEMATICS IN STYLE

The examples of science were always IN. Expecting you buy any garment in this persevering through style one year, you ought to have conviction that the next year it will despite be correspondingly sweet. They have been at the top for a few seasons and it is more than sure that they will not just leave style. Facilitators come a titanic number of years with new plans that will liven up any storeroom. Numerical shapes can help ladies with cautiously covering a piece of the inadequacies. They can be a wearisome time of recovery for men. Uncommon brocades and undying frameworks are a sensible choice for vivifying your wardrobe.

The best imaginative utilization of numerical models in visual computerization Numerical models has a surprising ability to dazzle. They are exact and capable, yet they can in this way show up, evidently, to be liquid and reliably moving. All through the range of time, this mix of plan and headway ought to be clear in planning and workmanship. In a numerical model, a lot of lines and shapes are repeated in a coordinated way. Whether you use a simple shape or a tangled modernized plan, the common eye typically believes that it is connecting with.

Numerical models can be used in visual representation to maintain class while also making a setting more pleasant. In this blog, we will look at a few examples of how mathematical models can be used to show things visually. Knowing how to plan mathematical models is key. if you significantly have any desire to send off an Integral propelling effort or make a staggering brand wonderful.

NUMERICAL GAME-PLAN SHAPES FOR BRAND CHARACTER STRUCTURES

Numerical models can be used to make stunning visual characters for brands. You can choose from a wide range of designs, colors, and sizes that are perfect for the brand. You can make tenacious minor takeoff from the models by consistent use of the picked shapes and game plans. Whenever you have spread out the brand character structure, you can use it to design the site, logo, business cards, limited application, and amazingly more. On the other hand, shape brain science expects to play a significant role, just as assortment brain science is used to influence client decisions during development. Here is a quick rundown of the most fundamental shapes for numerical arrangement. Circles Delicacy is tended to by curving edges and evolving shapes. Additionally, the sense of community, creativity, and closeness.

Triangles

Pointed edges and different sorts of triangles propose movement, power, heading, and advancement.

Squares or Square shapes

Related with plans and plan. Discuss requesting, consistency, and stability.

BRAND LOGO PLAN WITH CLEAR MATH

The logo is irrefutably the central piece of brand character and computation can expect to be a crucial part here. Logos of a brand are associated with the brand's most significant anticipated benefits. It is used in each euphoric and thing packaging. You can make similarly engaging moderate and rich plans by utilizing the direct mathematical model. Consider the most incontrovertible brands and their most recent logos. YouTube, Spotify, and Adidas, for example all of them obviously use numerical shapes. These brand logos are easy to audit for the social event. The arrangement that is misrepresented focuses on brands.

NUMERICAL MODELS FOR THINGS AND PACKAGING

Right when the brand logo and character are conceptualized, you can moreover recall numerical models for things and packaging. In point of fact, the use of mathematical models in configuration has become extremely modern with contemporary brands. You will see subjects recorded as a printed form material things and home style things an exceptional arrangement. Make-up brands and importance things can similarly stand disconnected with striking plans. The final touch is thing bundling. Numerical models can make sharp and immaculate plans that resonate with your picture.

USE EVALUATION IN DECREASED APPLICATIONS AND SITE PLAN

Astonishing UI/UX is the most raised need of moderate applications and complaints. As an originator, you would have to make the arrangement super-easy to explore and at the same time, you don't thoroughly recognize that the client ought to get depleted. Besides, the best method for making your modernized arrangement stand separated is to use numerical models. Spill Make Your Web based Game Stand Apart Clear mathematical course of action models can likewise make your internet game stick out. We overall in all know the hurried significance of standing separated through virtual redirection stages, especially Instagram and Facebook. As another business or brand, you ought to zero in on making major areas of strength for a personality.

Numerical models can be used to make the best story plans and attracting fulfilled for your social event. Broadcasting an arrangement or the farewell of something different? Use the power of evaluation.

Utilizing Mathematical Models to Consider Signs and Different Variables Mathematical models most certainly can possibly take care of all of your game plan issues. In any case, when you recall them for your course of action, you should rehearse alert. Size and degree matter. Essentially, a relative time, tremendous procedures for are being innovative. In any event, check out at the going with tips.

1. Make offset with blend and plan: If you are using a light model with fundamental shapes, supplement it with conveying energy. Fundamentally, if you are making a huge model, use essential insightful styles to change the effect. Balance is major, regardless of what the kind of plan you set up.

2. Look out for esteem: The vital a piece of math is this. Whether you are using isometric triangles or a mix of different models, change them as shown by balance. Your plan will be incredibly enamoring accordingly.

3. Interface your models with the subject: While making arrangements, you ought to never overlook the subject. There might be a reason for each line and shape. If it's a food business, you can use colors like yellow and red, which have been shown to make people need more, with shapes that are associated with the things.

4. Move past plans with pictures: With pictures, arranging shapes can become significantly more appealing. Edges and assortments can be made by utilizing shapes. Again, make it a priority to make it even and different.

5. Balance is stunning: The best perspective with respect to mathematical models is the means by which they can really make your game plan stick out. Precisely when a prompt triangle with a staggering text style can finish the work, there is persuading clarification need to make things more tangled.

6. Joining typography with plans: Your typography and text styles can be extremely beneficial to your numerical models. We have seen text style producers play with computation to make amazing creative styles. Fashioners can other than mix their models with imaginative styles.

HOW MIGHT YOU MAKE MATHEMATICAL MODELS FOR YOUR PLANS ON ENHANCE?

You really need an unfathomable instrument since it has turned out to be so clear how to incorporate mathematical models for checking! Improved is a no matter what your viewpoint game plan instrument that is easy to use and has all the numerical blueprint parts that you could require. You can find a ton of facilitated plans with attracting gathering ranges and numerical models. Feel free to change them to form your exceptional strategy. Begin with for all intents and purposes no proposing to make something totally exceptional. Investigate cutting-edge media like the most recent fonts, stickers, and visual elements. Moreover, you can change your material for different stages. You can correspondingly plan the most enthralling standards and flag content with a couple of fundamental snaps. Share straightforwardly or download in awesome. Cooperate to organize your number one applications effectively.

CHAPTER FOUR

HOW MATHEMATICAL OUTLINES MAKE ARRANGEMENT MODELS

Shapes are some different option from a variety of related lines. It is used in bits of pictures and plans. They pass on a particular message or interpreting that you don't know anything about. Fundamentally a square, circle and triangle in an arrangement have an impact of what you could think from it. It brings out feeling, mindset, improvement, and thought depiction. They are assembled under the social occasion of numerical shapes and are consolidated models that are really undeniable by us. It could have all of the stores of being just a fundamental shape that even a kindergarten youth would know. In any case, there are various explanations behind their discernible quality.

Headway cheating: What makes the development a head honcho part? The numerical organized bit of each building interlocks to gain a deceptive of headway. The usage strong regions for of is changed by structure a wave improvement. The entire idea causes a plan to have all of the stores of being moving rather than static.

Numerical Outlines There are no limitations on how numerical representations can be managed. Take a look at one of the most notable examples of using mathematical images as both covers and gifts. A blend of chief shapes, light surface and certain gathering makes a layered and striking portrayal. In case you're adequately gutsy, empower an image of yourself with these three direct parts.

Upgrade The way that several mathematical shapes charge up is a mind blowing part. They are considered as shapes that are repeated with basically no openings or covering. Have a go at interlocking them to shape a fundamental line that directs the eyes to a particular course. Right when the shapes are gotten along with pictures or articles that conform to each part, it will have characteristics for a

Keep It Pointless Many have explanation "calming could be great", what do they unequivocally mean by that? Balance may be one of the most appealing planning styles of today. By only using the components that are crucial to a particular arrangement, this is accomplished. Shapes and models ought to be simple and less difficult to understand. This is to alter the various components of the arrangement.

Delicate Model Without using striking shapes, an arrangement can withstand exposure. Mathematical shapes that are delicate and delicate can, without a doubt, be just as useful and creative as ones that are more solid and refined. It helps with keeping an arrangement great, rich and master. It isn't needed for each arrangement to recognizably feature your model. In like manner, it suits more in corporate venturing, for instance, name cards and proceeds.

Numerical Slant One more method for integrating a numerical model into a marketable strategy is to utilize a tendency. A striking procedure for making it look inconspicuous and smooth is to utilize an arrive at that is apparently a grade. Offer it a chance in the following task you work on.

NUMERICAL NEGATIVE SHAPES

Negative space is the space around and between subjects of an image. It becomes perceivable when it pushes toward an enchanting gigantic shape. It will deal with the qualification and provide an extraordinary and charming edge when you combine mathematical models and images. Negative shapes and parcel need to work nicely together as they are coordinated in a way to put forth watcher's organized attempt in checking the various parts out. Adding second visual interest is the best technique for catching the watcher's advantage. There's nothing uncommonly debilitating as zeroing in on an irrefutable piece of plain tones. Your plan gains visual interest thanks to mathematical models. You will not have the option to oppose the outcome on the off chance that you orchestrate the different mathematical model ideas in a deliberate way.

THE END